THE KAMADO GRILL COOKBOOK

Complete Smoker Cookbook to Smoke and Grill Full-Flavor Meat, Fish, Game, Vegetable Recipes with Your Ceramic Cooker

By Roger Murphy

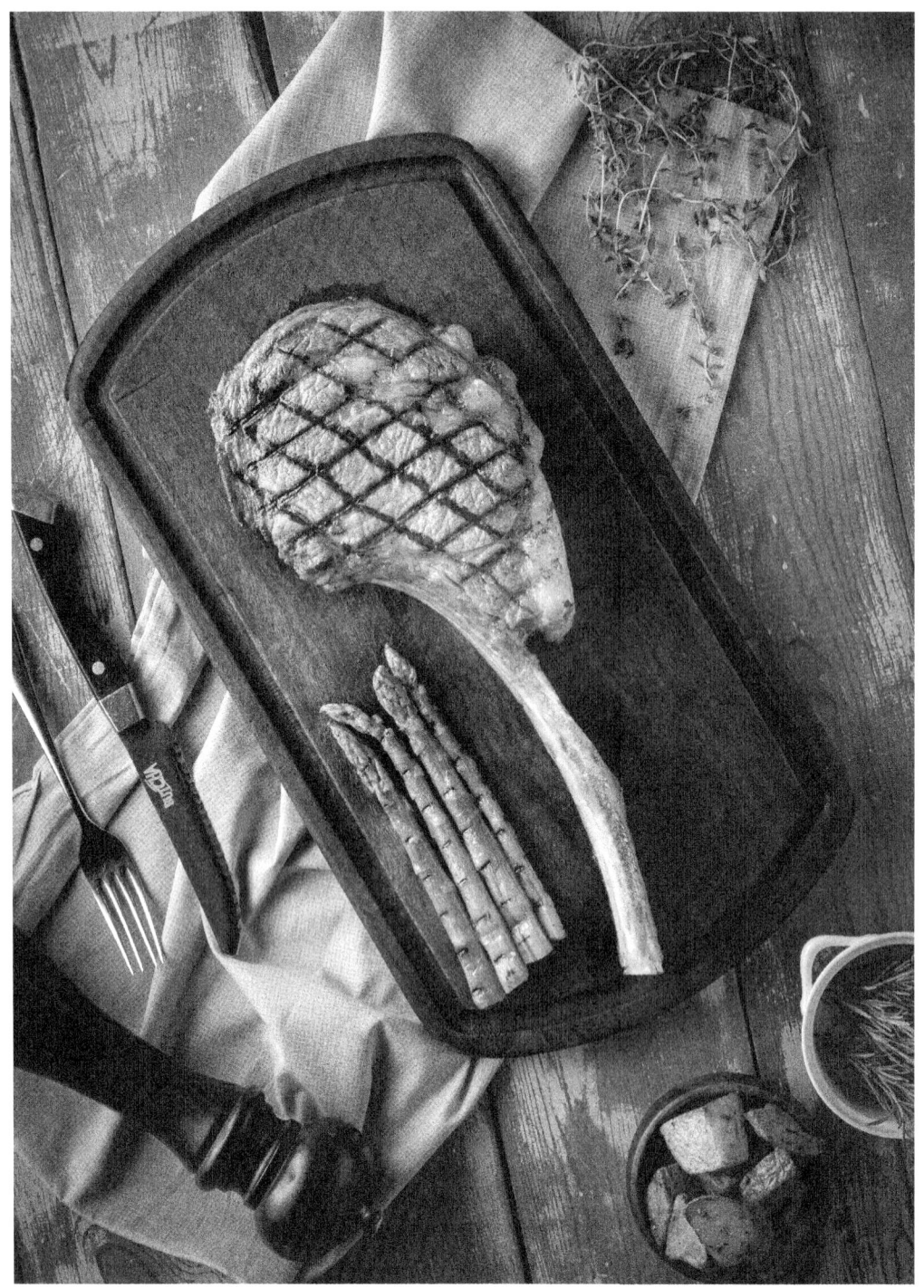

TABLE OF CONTENTS

INTRODUCTION 9

CHAPTER-1 BEEF 10
- BBQ ROAST BEEF 11
- BEER-BRAISED BEEF RIBS 13
- HICKORY MAPLE BEEF JERKY 16
- PIMENTO CHEESEBURGERS 19
- TOAD IN THE HOLE 22

CHAPTER-2 PORK 24
- BAKED LINGUINE WITH ITALIAN SAUSAGE 25
- PEACH BRINED PORK LOIN WITH BACON AND GARDEN VEGETABLES 28
- PIGS IN A BLANKET 31
- PULLED PORK SHOULDER 34
- SWEET AND SMOKY PULLED PORK SANDWICHES 37
- TWO CHEESE AND BACON DIP 40

CHAPTER-3 HAM 43
- HAM AND CHEESE PANINI 44
- HAM HOCKS AND COLLARD GREENS 46
- SMOKED HAM FRITTATA 49

CHAPTER-4 LAMB 52

BBQ LAMB CHOPS 53

GRILLED LEG OF LAMB WITH GARLIC AND ROSEMARY 55

PIZZA WITH SPICY LAMB AND TOMATOES 57

POMEGRANATE AND CRANBERRY-MARINATED RACK OF LAMB 60

SPICY LAMB SKEWERS 63

CHAPTER-5 CHICKEN 66

BBQ CHICKEN WITH ASIAN DIPPING SAUCE 67

CHICKEN SKEWERS 69

GRILLED CHICKEN SALAD 72

PISTACHIO CHICKEN 75

CHAPTER-6 TURKEY 78

SMOKED TURKEY 79

SOUTHWEST-STYLE TURKEY BURGERS 82

TURKEY BACON DOGS 84

TURKEY POTATO SKINS 86

CHAPTER-7 FISH 89

BLACKENED CAJUN CATFISH 90

GRILLED ASIAN SALMON 92

GRILLED RED SNAPPER IN BANANA LEAVES 94

MAHI MAHI 97

CHAPTER-8 SEAFOOD 99

- BBQ SHRIMP SALAD 100
- LOBSTER ROLLS 103
- NEW ENGLAND STYLE CLAM CHOWDER 106
- SMOKED CRAB DIP 109

CHAPTER-9 GAME 111

- BEAR BURGERS 112
- GRILLED HONEY-GLAZE CORNISH HENS 114
- HONEY-ORANGE MARINADED GATOR KEBABS 116
- SMOKED GOOSE 119

CHAPTER-10 VEGGIES 122

- BACON-WRAPPED ONION RINGS 122
- BRUSSELS SPROUTS AU GRATIN 124
- CREAMY CHEESE POTATO SALAD 127
- GRILLED ARTICHOKES WITH LEMON DILL YOGURT SAUCE 130
- MEXICAN STREET CORN 133

CHAPTER-11 CERAMIC GILL 136

- Different Sizes of Kamado Grills 136
- Ceramic Grill Tips 138

Cooking Types 139
- Direct Grilling 139
- Indirect Grilling 139
- Smoking 140
- Baking 140

CHAPTER-12 SMOKING TIPS AND TRICKS 141
- Selecting a Smoker 141
- Choose your wood 141
- Find the right temperature 143
- The core difference between cold and hot smoking 143
- The basic preparations 144
- The core elements of smoking! 145

CONCLUSION 146

MY BOOKS 147

Get Your FREE Gift 154

INTRODUCTION

Smoking is generally used as one of the cooking methods nowadays. The food enriches in protein such as meat would spoil quickly, if cooked for a longer period of time with modern cooking techniques. Whereas, Smoking is a low & slow process of cooking the meat. Where there is a smoke, there is a flavor. With white smoke, you can boost the flavor of your food. In addition to this statement, you can preserve the nutrition present in the food as well. This is flexible & one of the oldest techniques of making food. It's essential for you to brush the marinade over your food while you cook and let the miracle happen. The only thing you need to do is to add a

handful of fresh coals or wood chips as and when required. Just taste your regular grilled meat and a smoked meat, you yourself would find the difference.

Remember one thing i.e. "Smoking is an art". With a little time & practice, even you can become an expert. Once you become an expert with smoking technique, believe me, you would never look for other cooking techniques. To find one which smoking technique works for you, you must experiment with different woods & cooking methods. Just cook the meat over indirect heat source & cook it for hours. When smoking your meats, it's very important that you let the smoke to escape & move around.

CHAPTER-1 BEEF

· CUTS OF BEEF ·

BBQ ROAST BEEF

(TOTAL COOK TIME 3 HOURS 10 MINUTES)

INGREDIENTS FOR 2 SERVINGS

THE MEAT

- 1 beef joint (3.3-lb, 1.5-kg)
- BBQ marinade, store-bought, of choice – ½ cup
- Salt and freshly ground black pepper

THE KAMADO GRILL

- Heat the grill for indirect cooking to 400°F (204°C)

METHOD

1. Add the beef joint to a ziplock bag.
2. Pour the marinade into the bag and transfer to the fridge for 2-3 hours. You will need to turn the meat over while in the bag occasionally.
3. When you are ready to beginning grilling, season the meat liberally with salt and freshly ground black pepper.
4. Cook the meat for 15 minutes per (1-lb, 0.45-kg) for around 50-60 minutes.
5. Serve and enjoy.

BEER-BRAISED BEEF RIBS

(TOTAL COOK TIME 2 HOURS 20 MINUTES)

INGREDIENTS FOR 3-4 SERVINGS

THE MEAT

- Beef short ribs, sliced into individual ribs (5-lb, 2.3-kg)

THE INGREDIENTS

- Yellow onion, peeled and diced large – 3 cups
- Carrots, diced – 1 cup
- 1 head of garlic cloves, peeled and crushed
- Chipotle in adobo sauce – ½ cup
- BBQ rub – 3 tablespoons
- 5-6 cans beer, as needed
- Honey mustard, as needed
- BBQ rub, as needed

THE KAMADO GRILL

- When the internal temperature of the ribs reach around 200°F (93°F), build a hot charcoal fire in the grill
- Heat the grill for direct grilling with the airflow wide open on the top and the bottom. The desired temperature is 500°F (260°C)

METHOD

1. Add the onion, carrots, garlic, chipotles, 3 tablespoons of rub, and the beef ribs to a Dutch oven of 7-quart capacity.
2. Pour in sufficient beer to cover the ingredients.
3. Cover the Dutch oven with a lid.
4. Bring the ingredients to a boil before turning the heat down to low and maintaining a gentle simmer.
5. Cook the ribs until they are probe-tender and reach an internal temperature of around 207°F (97°C). This process should take around 2 hours.
6. Heat the grill for direct grilling as instructed.
7. Once the ribs are probe tender, remove them from the Dutch oven, and pat dry using kitchen paper towels.
8. Slather a generous amount of honey mustard over the ribs, season with BBQ rub, and quickly grill over the hot charcoal to lightly char.
9. Serve and enjoy.

HICKORY MAPLE BEEF JERKY

(TOTAL COOK TIME 11 HOUR 10 MINUTES)

INGREDIENTS FOR 2-3 SERVINGS

THE MEAT

- Silverside of beef or eye of round, fat removed (2-lb, 0.9-kg)

THE DRY CURE

- Maple syrup – ¼ cup
- Worcestershire sauce – ¼ cup
- Dried oregano – 1 teaspoon
- Freshly ground black pepper – 1 teaspoon
- Ancho chili powder – 1 teaspoon
- Garlic powder – ½ teaspoon
- Onion powder – ½ teaspoon
- Flaky sea salt – 1⅗ teaspoons
- Pink curing salt – ⅙ tsp

THE KAMADO GRILL

- Heat the Kamado grill for indirect cooking to 160-175°F (70-80°C)
- You will need 1 small chunk of hickory wood

METHOD

1. When you have successfully removed all the fat from the meat, transfer to the freezer until slightly firm but not frozen.
2. Slice the meat into strips against the grain. The strips should be 0.12-in (4-mm) wide.
3. Combine the cure ingredients in a bowl (maple syrup, Worcestershire sauce, oregano, black pepper, chili powder, garlic powder, onion powder, sea salt, and curing salt).
4. Add the meat to the bowl, combine and transfer to the fridge for 8 hours.
5. When you are ready to begin cooking, smoke the meat strips over hickory wood for around 3-4 hours. You can do this by placing the meat strips on a rack.
6. Smoke the meat until nearly all of the moisture has gone from the beef.
7. Remove from the Kamado grill and store in an airtight container.

PIMENTO CHEESEBURGERS

(TOTAL COOK TIME 25 MINUTES)

INGREDIENTS FOR 6 SERVINGS

THE MEAT

- Ground beef/brisket (2-lb, 0.9-kg)
- Butter, as needed
- Beef BBQ rub, as needed

THE SPREAD

- Mature yellow Cheddar cheese, grated (4-oz, 113-gm)
- Horseradish Cheddar, grated (4-oz, 113-gm)
- Cream cheese, room temperature (2-oz, 57-gm)
- Canned or jarred diced pimentos, rinsed (2-oz, 57-gm)
- Mayonnaise – ¼ cup
- Dijon mustard – 1½ teaspoons
- Hot sauce, of choice – 1½ teaspoons
- Worcestershire sauce – 1½ teaspoons
- Fresh chives, minced – 1½ teaspoons

THE INGREDIENTS

- 6 brioche buns
- 6 bacon slices
- Butter lettuce leaves
- Garlic dill pickles, as needed
- 2-3 tomatoes, thinly sliced

THE KAMADO GRILL

- Build a hot coal base to a stable temperature of 450-500°F (232-260°C)
- Push the coals to one side
- Position a half-moon grill grate panel on the grate at the lower setting over the hot coals
- On the cool side of the Kamado grill, position a half moon cast iron griddle at the highest setting

METHOD

1. First, prepare the pimento spread. In a bowl, combine the yellow Cheddar, horseradish Cheddar, cream cheese, pimentos, mayonnaise, Dijon mustard, hot sauce, Worcestershire sauce, and chives. Mix thoroughly until incorporated.
2. Divide the ground beef into 6 even-size patties and transfer to the fridge until you are ready to begin grilling.
3. Add butter to the grill and toast the buns.
4. Cook the bacon on the griddle. Remove the bacon and transfer to a plate.
5. Season the patties with beef rub.
6. Arrange the seasoned patties on the half-moon grill grate panel and grill until grill marks appear on both sides. Cook until their internal temperature reaches around 140°F (60°C). After which, transfer them to the griddle.
7. Top each burger with ¼ cup of the pimento spread from Step 1.
8. Continue to grill the patties until they reach an internal temperature of 155°F (68°C). Remove the patties from the griddle.
9. Next, assemble the burgers. Place a lettuce leaf on the bottom half of each brioche bun. Top with a pickle and slices of fresh tomato. Lay the cheeseburger on top, followed by the bacon, remaining pimento spread, and top half of the bun.
10. Serve and enjoy.

TOAD IN THE HOLE

(TOTAL COOK TIME 45 MINUTES)

INGREDIENTS FOR 4 SERVINGS

THE MEAT

- 12 premium-quality sausages

THE YORKSHIRE PUDDING

- Flour (5-oz, 142-gm)
- 1 large egg
- 1 large egg white
- Milk – 1 cup
- A pinch of salt
- Vegetable oil – 2 tablespoons

THE KAMADO GRILL

- Set the Kamado grill for direct cooking and cook the sausages as directed below
- When the sausages are cooked, insert the heat deflector stones and reset the grill for indirect cooking and stabilize the temperature to 350°F (177°C)
- Position an oven tray greased with oil in the Kamado grill for approximately 5 minutes and allow to reach the smoke point, and continue with Step 4 of the method instructions

METHOD

1. First, sift the flour into a bowl.
2. Add the egg, and egg white, followed by a splash of milk into the flour, and whisk. Continue adding the milk and the salt and oil, and whisk until a thick batter-like consistency.
3. Grill the sausages for 15 minutes, until browned lightly. When cooked through, remove the sausages from the grill and set aside.
4. Lay the sausages quickly in a line in the oven tray.
5. Pour the batter over the sausages.
6. Close the Kamado grill, and bake at 350°F (177°C) for 20 minutes while taking care not to lift the lid.
7. Serve the sausages with the Yorkshire pudding and enjoy.

CHAPTER-2 PORK

· CUTS OF PORK ·

BAKED LINGUINE WITH ITALIAN SAUSAGE

(TOTAL COOK TIME 1 HOUR 45 MINUTES)

INGREDIENTS FOR 8 SERVINGS

THE MEAT

- 4 Italian pork sausages
- Nonstick cooking spray

THE INGREDIENTS

- Linguine (8-oz, 226-gm)
- 2 eggs
- Italian 6-cheese blend, shredded and divided– 3 cups
- 1 jar store-bought spaghetti sauce (24-oz, 680-gm)

THE KAMADO GRILL

- Heat the grill for direct cooking to 350°F (177°C)

METHOD

1. Spritz the inside of an 8-in (20-cm) oven-safe baking dish with nonstick cooking spray.
2. Add the sausages to the grill and grill until cooked through. Put to one side.
3. Add the pasta to a pan filled with boiling water, and cook until al dente. Drain the pasta and rinse under cold running water.
4. In a small bowl, beat the eggs.
5. Add the beaten eggs to the cooked pasta and combine.
6. To the egg and pasta, stir in 1 cup of shredded Italian cheese. Spoon the mixture into the prepared baking dish.
7. Slice the cooked sausages into quarters, and arrange them on top of the pasta mixture.
8. Pour the store-bought sauce evenly over the top.
9. Add the heat deflector racks and plates to the Kamado grill for indirect cooking.
10. Uncovered, place the baking dish in the grill and cook for 30 minutes.
11. Remove from the grill and top with 2 cups of shredded Italian cheese, and bake for 25-30 minutes, until browned lightly.
12. Allow to stand for 8-10 minutes before serving.

PEACH BRINED PORK LOIN WITH BACON AND GARDEN VEGETABLES

(TOTAL COOK TIME 11 HOUR 30 MINUTES)

INGREDIENTS FOR 10 SERVINGS

THE MEAT

- Pork loin (4-lb, 1.8-kg)

THE BRINE

- Peach nectar (24-oz, 680-gm)
- Coarsely ground sea salt - ½ cup
- Dark brown sugar – ½ cup
- Water (12-oz, 340-gm)

THE INGREDIENTS

- 3 slices bacon, cut into thirds
- 1 whole onion, peeled and quartered
- 8 whole white mushrooms, halved
- 12 stalks asparagus, trimmed
- Olive oil, as needed
- Kosher salt, as needed
- Freshly ground black pepper, as needed
- Peach jam (4-oz, 113-gm)

THE KAMADO GRILL

- Heat the grill for indirect cooking to 225°F (107°C)

METHOD

1. In a pot, combine the peach nectar, salt, brown sugar, and water while stirring. Bring to a boil and remove the pot from the heat. Cover with a lid, and allow the mixture to brine and cool to room temperature.
2. Add the meat to a ziplock bag.
3. Pour the brine into the bag and transfer to the fridge overnight.
4. Remove the pork loin from the brine, rinse with cold water, and using kitchen paper towels, pat dry.
5. Brush a cast-iron skillet with a splash of oil.
6. Lay the pork, fat side facing down in the skillet.
7. Arrange the bacon, onion, mushrooms, and asparagus around the meat. Brush all over with oil and season the veggies with salt and black pepper.
8. Next, around 30-45 minutes, before removing the meat from the grill, brush the surface of the pork with peach jam. Cook until the meat registers an internal temperature of 145-160°F (63-71°C). The total cooking time is around 2 hours 30 minutes.
9. Remove the meat from the Kamado grill and tent loosely with foil for 10 minutes.
10. Slice, serve, and enjoy.

PIGS IN A BLANKET

(TOTAL COOK TIME 1 HOUR)

INGREDIENTS FOR 24 SERVINGS

THE MEAT

- 24 mini cocktail franks

THE INGREDIENTS

- 1 dill pickle, quartered
- 12 pickled sport peppers
- 1 can crescent roll dough (12-oz, 340-gm)
- Celery salt – 1 tablespoon
- 1 egg
- Water – 1 tablespoon
- Poppy seeds – 2 tablespoons
- Mustard, to dip

THE KAMADO GRILL

- Heat the grill for indirect cooking and stabilize to 375°F (190°C)

METHOD

1. First, slice the dill pickle spears into 24 pieces (6 per spear). They should be a bit wider than a matchstick and around 1-in (2.54-cm) than the mini franks.
2. Slice the sports peppers in half or until they are the same size as the dill pickle pieces.

3. Open the can of crescent roll and place the dough on a clean, plastic board or work surface.
4. Using a pizza cutter and a ruler, cut the dough into even-sized strips.
5. Lay the rectangle of dough on the work surface and from top to bottom, cut into 12 slices. Next, make a single cut from the left to across the middle of the dough to create 24 slices.
6. Season the dough with celery salt to cover, but not clump.
7. Line a baking sheet or pizza pan with parchment paper.
8. With the celery salt seasoned side of a dough slice facing upwards, place a sport pepper piece followed by a pickle sliver and a mini frank approximately 0.5-in (1.28-cm) up from the bottom edge.
9. Start by rolling the dough up around the filling. It will do this approximately 1½ times. It is okay if the ends of the hot dogs are exposed.
10. Arrange the bundles on the prepared baking sheet, seam side facing down. Repeat the process with the remaining ingredients to make 24 bundles.
11. In a bowl, beat the egg with water to create an egg wash. Brush the wash all over the dough areas and scatter over the poppy seeds.
12. Place the baking sheet or pan on the preheated grill and cook until golden brown for 10-12 minutes.
13. Serve with your favorite dipping sauce or mustard and enjoy.

PULLED PORK SHOULDER

(TOTAL COOK TIME 5-8 HOURS)

INGREDIENTS FOR 8 SERVINGS

THE MEAT

- Boston butt pork shoulder (10-lb, 4.5-kg)
- Tangy and sweet BBQ sauce, as needed
- BBQ rub, as needed

THE SAUCE

- Apple cider vinegar – 2 cups
- Ketchup – ½ cup
- Brown sugar – ¼ cup
- Sea salt – 4 teaspoons
- Crushed red pepper – 2 teaspoons

THE KAMADO GRILL

- Build a large charcoal base, and stabilize the temperature to 300°F (149°C)
- Add 2 large chunks of pecan wood to the charcoal

METHOD

1. Trim the surface tissue from the pork butt's crevice, taking care not to cut the meat.
2. Rub a fine layer of BBQ sauce over the surface of the meat and season liberally with BBQ rub.
3. Place the meat on the grill and serve for 60 minutes before mopping.
4. To prepare the sauce, in a 4 cup size Mason jar, combine vinegar, ketchup, sugar, sea salt, and red pepper in a Mason jar of 4 cup capacity. Seal the jar with a lid and shake well. Set some of the sauce aside.
5. Mop the meat with the sauce every 60 minutes until the meat is tender and pulls away from the bone. The meat is ready when it registers an internal temperature of 205°F (96°C).
6. When the meat is cool enough to easily handle, by hand, shred the meat. Remove the fat cap and dice into bite-size pieces, and combine into the shredded pork.
7. Serve with the sauce, set aside earlier in Step 4.
8. Enjoy.

SWEET AND SMOKY PULLED PORK SANDWICHES

(TOTAL COOK TIME 14 HOURS 30 MINUTES)

INGREDIENTS FOR 18 SERVINGS

THE MEAT

- 1 pork neck (5.5-lb, 2.5-kgs)

THE RUB

- Brown sugar – 10 tablespoons
- Onion powder – 3 tablespoons
- Turmeric – 2 tablespoons
- Cayenne pepper – 1½ tablespoons
- Garlic powder – 3 tablespoons
- Salt – 7 tablespoons
- Paprika – 7 tablespoons

THE SANDWICHES

- BBQ sauce
- 18 soft rolls
- Coleslaw, for serving

THE SMOKE

- Soak a large handful of cherry wood in water. Add a few handfuls of unsoaked cherry wood to the unlit charcoal. Open the draft door and arrange three fire starters over the charcoal and light. Keep the lid open for 10 minutes.
- Sprinkle the soaked cherry wood over the now-glowing charcoal. Set up the convector and arrange a grid inside.

METHOD

1. First, prepare the rub. Combine the sugar, onion powder, turmeric, cayenne pepper, garlic powder, salt, and paprika.
2. Cover the outside of the meat with the rub.
3. Arrange the pork on the grid and heat the kamdo to a temperature of 220°F (105°C). Cook the pork for approximately 8 hours until it registers an internal temperature of 160°F (70°C).
4. Remove the meat from the grill and wrap in aluminum foil. Return to the grill and cook for another several hours until it registers an internal temperature of 195°F (90°C).
5. Take the meat off the grill and allow to rest in the foil for another few hours.
6. Shred the cooled pork and toss in BBQ sauce.
7. Serve inside soft rolls topped with coleslaw.

TWO CHEESE AND BACON DIP

(TOTAL COOK TIME 1 HOUR 15 MINUTES)

INGREDIENTS FOR 15 SERVINGS

THE MEAT

- Bacon, cooked, and crumbled – ½ cup

THE INGREDIENTS

- Cream cheese, room temperature (1-lb, 0.45-kg)
- Mayonnaise – 1 cup
- Cayenne pepper – ½ teaspoon
- 2 shallots, chopped
- Sharp Cheddar cheese, shredded (8-oz, 226-gm)
- Parmesan cheese, shredded (6-oz, 170-gm)
- Butter, melted – 2 tablespoons
- Italian seasoned breadcrumbs – ½ cup

THE KAMADO GRILL

- Heat the grill for indirect cooking to 375°F (190°C)

METHOD

1. Combine the cream cheese, mayonnaise, and cayenne pepper in a bowl, and mix to incorporate.
2. To the mixture, add the shallots, Cheddar, and Parmesan cheeses to combine.
3. Spoon the mixture into an oven-safe baking dish.
4. Melt the butter and mix well with the breadcrumbs. Add the mixture to the top of the cheeses.
5. Place the dish on the grill and cook for around 40-45 minutes until the surface of the dip browns lightly.
6. Remove the dip from the grill and top with crumbled bacon.
7. Serve and enjoy with tortilla chips or crackers.

CHAPTER-3 HAM

HAM AND CHEESE PANINI

(TOTAL COOK TIME 10 MINUTES)

INGREDIENTS FOR 4 SERVINGS

THE MEAT

- Deli-sliced smoked ham (8-oz, 226-gm)

THE INGREDIENTS

- Spicy brown mustard – ¼ cup
- 8 slices brown bread
- 8 slices sharp white Cheddar cheese
- Baby arugula, packed – 2 cups
- 1 ripe Bartlett pear, cut into 20 slices, cored
- Olive oil, as needed

THE KAMADO GRILL

- Heat the grill for direct cooking to 400°F (204°C)
- Add and preheat a half moon cast iron griddle, ridged side facing upwards

METHOD

1. Spread the brown mustard over one side of each bread slice.
2. Top each of the four bread slices with one slice of Cheddar cheese followed by half of the arugula. Next, add the pear and deli ham slices.
3. Press the sandwiches together slightly, and brush the outside with oil.
4. Cook the sandwiches on the griddle, flipping over once until the cheese is melted and the bread is browned.
5. Serve.

HAM HOCKS AND COLLARD GREENS

(TOTAL COOK TIME 1 HOUR 20 MINUTES)

INGREDIENTS FOR 8 SERVINGS

THE MEAT

- 2 ham hocks (2-lb, 0.9-kg)

THE INGREDIENTS

- 1 large yellow onion, peeled and diced large
- 1 large carrot, trimmed and diced large
- 3 garlic cloves, peeled and crushed
- 3 sprigs fresh thyme
- 1 bay leaf
- A pinch of red chili flakes
- Water – 16 cups

THE COLLARD GREENS

- Chili-infused oil, any brand – 2 tablespoons
- 1 medium yellow onion, peeled and sliced
- Tri-tip seasoning, any brand – 1 tablespoon
- Garlic, peeled and minced – 2 tablespoons
- Collard greens, rinsed, ribs removed, and leaves sliced to 0.5-in (1.27-cm) thick, total weight (2-lb, 0.9-kg)
- Apple cider vinegar – ¼ cup
- Brown sugar – ¼ cup
- Smoked salt, as needed, to season

THE KAMADO GRILL

- Build a large hotbed of coals, heat for direct cooking and stabilize to 425°F (218°C)

METHOD

1. In a Dutch oven of 7-quart capacity, combine the ham hock with onion, carrot, garlic, thyme, bay leaf, and red chili flakes.
2. Pour in the water, and simmer until the meat pulls away from the bone and liquid is reduced to around 2 cups. This step will take 1 hour 30 minutes to 2 hours. Strain the liquid and pull the ham from the bones.
3. Discard the ham bones along with the connective tissue and skin. Chop the meat and put to one side. Add the strained liquid to a container, and set to one side also.
4. Return the now-empty Dutch oven to the Kamado grill.
5. Add the chili-infused oil to the Dutch oven, followed by the onions and tri-tip seasoning. Cook until the onions are translucent.
6. Next, add the garlic and cook for another 60 seconds.
7. Add the collard greens followed by the diced ham and ham stock liquid, set aside earlier. Cook until the greens are bite-tender, for approximately 30 minutes.
8. Pour in the vinegar and add the brown sugar. Stir to dissolve, and taste and season with smoked salt.
9. Serve and enjoy.

SMOKED HAM FRITTATA

(TOTAL COOK TIME 30 MINUTES)

INGREDIENTS FOR 4 SERVINGS

THE MEAT

- Smoked ham, chopped – 2 cups
- Extra-virgin olive oil – 2 tablespoons
- Butter – 3 tablespoons

THE INGREDIENTS

- Sweet onion, minced – ½ cup
- 1 leek, top removed, rinsed, and chopped
- 2 russet potatoes, peeled and chopped small
- Salt – 1 teaspoon
- Black pepper – 1 teaspoon
- 8 whole eggs
- Heavy cream – 1 cup
- Cheddar cheese, shredded - ½ cup
- Goat cheese, crumbled - ½ cup

THE KAMADO GRILL

- Heat the grill for indirect cooking to 400°F (204°C)
- Add and preheat a skillet

METHOD

1. Heat the oil and butter in the skillet.
2. Once the fats melt, add the onion, leek, and potatoes. Season the veggies with salt and black pepper. Cook while occasionally stirring until the leeks and onion have sweated down, and the potatoes are fork-tender. This process will take around 12-15 minutes.
3. Spread the veggie mixture evenly on the bottom of the skillet.
4. Meanwhile, whisk the eggs, cream, and Cheddar cheese in a bowl.
5. Add the egg mixture followed by the ham to the skillet and cook for 10 minutes.
6. Next, scatter the goat cheese over the surface of the mixture and cook for an additional 10 minutes until the center of the frittata sets and the edges are golden.
7. Slide carefully onto a plate, and set aside to rest for 8-10 minutes before slicing and serving.

CHAPTER-4 LAMB

· CUTS OF LAMB ·

BBQ LAMB CHOPS

(TOTAL COOK TIME 50 MINUTES)

INGREDIENTS FOR 4 SERVINGS

THE MEAT

- 8-12 lamb chops

THE MARINADE

- Red currant jelly – 2 tablespoons
- Tomato ketchup – 2 tablespoons
- Reduced-sodium light soy sauce – 2 tablespoons
- Runny honey – 2 tablespoons
- Dry English mustard – 1 tablespoon
- Worcestershire sauce – 1 tablespoon

THE KAMADO GRILL

- Heat the grill for direct cooking to 350-450°F (177-232°C)

METHOD

1. Add the lamb chops to a shallow dish or bowl.
2. In a second bowl, combine the marinade ingredients, red currant jelly, ketchup, soy sauce, honey, mustard, and Worcestershire sauce, and mix to incorporate.
3. Pour the marinade over the lamb and set aside for 30 minutes. You do not need to place in the fridge.
4. Remove the chops from the marinade, shaking off any excess, and place on your grill over direct moderate heat, lid closed for 8-12 minutes, depending on the thickness of the meat. You will need to flip them over halfway through the cooking process. The meat is ready when it registers an internal temperature, for medium-rare at 130°F (54°C). If you prefer medium to well-done, increase the timings by around 5 minutes or more.
5. Remove the meat from the grill and set aside to rest for 5 minutes before serving.

GRILLED LEG OF LAMB WITH GARLIC AND ROSEMARY

(TOTAL COOK TIME 1 HOUR 15 MINUTES)

INGREDIENTS FOR 4 SERVINGS

THE MEAT

- 1 leg of lamb (4-6-lb, 1.8-2.7-kg)
- Salt and freshly cracked pepper, as needed, to season
- Garlic, peeled, and chopped, as needed, to season
- Fresh rosemary, chopped, as needed, to season

THE KAMADO GRILL

- Heat the grill for indirect cooking, using deflector plates, to 350°F (177°C)

METHOD

1. Season the lamb with salt, pepper, garlic, and rosemary.
2. Next, tie the leg of lamb with butcher's twine to help it retain its shape.
3. Place the leg of lamb directly on the grill. Cook for around 1-2 hours, or until the meat registers an internal temperature of 140°F (60°C).
4. Serve and enjoy.

PIZZA WITH SPICY LAMB AND TOMATOES

(TOTAL COOK TIME 50 MINUTES)

INGREDIENTS FOR 2 SERVINGS*

THE MEAT

- Ground lamb (8-oz, 126-gm)

THE INGREDIENTS

- Fontina, coarsely grated (4-oz, 113-gm)
- Mozzarella cheese, coarsely grated (2-oz, 56-gm)
- Extra-virgin olive oil, divided – 4 tablespoons
- 2 garlic cloves, peeled and minced
- 1 small onion, peeled and finely chopped
- Tomato paste – 1 tablespoon
- Plum tomatoes, peeled, seeded, and chopped
- Fresh parsley, chopped – 3 tablespoons
- Toasted pine nuts – 3 tablespoons
- A large pinch each of ground cinnamon, ground cloves, ground allspice
- Crushed red pepper - ⅛ teaspoon
- Salt and freshly ground black pepper to season
- Freshly squeezed lemon juice – 1-2 teaspoons
- Readymade pizza dough for two 9-in (23-cm) pizzas

THE KAMADO GRILL

- Heat the grill for indirect cooking to 500°F (260°C)
- Preheat a pizza and baking stone

METHOD

1. In a bowl, combine the grated fontina and grated mozzarella cheeses. Add 2 tablespoons of oil and minced garlic and set aside for 30 minutes.
2. In a large skillet, heat the remaining oil. Add the onions to the pan and sauté for 10 minutes until softened. Add the lamb, tomato paste, tomatoes, parsley, pine nuts, cinnamon, cloves, allspice, ¼ teaspoon salt, and ¼ teaspoon of pepper. Cook the meat slowly, uncovered for 10 minutes. Stir in the fresh lemon juice to combine.
3. On a floured worktop, halve the dough. Roll each half out into 0.25-in (0.64-cm) thick rounds. Transfer one piece of dough onto a generously floured pizza peel.
4. Brush the dough with garlic oil.
5. Scatter half of the grated cheeses over the top and spoon on half of the lamb mixture.
6. Transfer the pizza to the stone and cook until crisp and golden, for 8-10 minutes. Repeat the process for the second pizza.

*This recipe makes two 9-in (23-cm) pizzas

POMEGRANATE AND CRANBERRY-MARINATED RACK OF LAMB

(TOTAL COOK TIME 2 HOURS 25 MINUTES)

INGREDIENTS FOR 4-6 SERVINGS

THE MEAT

- 2 racks of lamb, Frenched

THE INGREDIENTS

- Pomegranate juice – 1 cup
- White or red wine – 1 cup
- Cranberries – ½ cup
- 1 sprig of fresh rosemary
- Salt and freshly ground black pepper, to season
- Olive oil – 2 tablespoons

THE KAMADO GRILL

- Heat the grill for direct cooking to 400°F (204°C)

METHOD

1. Place the racks of lamb in a large deep dish.
2. Pour in the pomegranate juice, wine (of choice), cranberries, and rosemary.
3. Cover the dish with a lid, and transfer to the fridge for 2-8 hours.
4. Remove the lamb from the marinade, and pat dry. Season the meat with salt and black pepper.
5. Add the marinade to a pan, and bring to a boil.
6. Turn the heat down, and simmer until a thin glaze consistency. Remove and discard the sprig of rosemary, and keep the glaze warm.
7. In a cast-iron skillet, heat the oil. Add the lamb to the skillet and sear on all sides to brown.
8. Remove the skillet from the grill.
9. Place the lamb rack on the grid and cook until medium-rare for 8-10 minutes.
10. Set aside to rest for 3-4 minutes before slicing into chops.
11. Serve and enjoy.

SPICY LAMB SKEWERS

(TOTAL COOK TIME 50 MINUTES)

INGREDIENTS FOR 6-8 SERVINGS

THE MEAT

- 1 lamb roast (2-lb, 0.9-kg)

THE RUB

- Cumin seeds – 3 tablespoons
- Black peppercorns – 1 tablespoon
- Dried chili flakes – 1 tablespoon
- Salt – 1 tablespoon
- Onion powder – 1½ teaspoons
- Garlic powder – ½ teaspoon

THE KAMADO GRILL

- Heat the grill for direct cooking to 450°F (232°C)
- You will need 6-8 metal skewers for this recipe

METHOD

1. In a small skillet, toast the cumin seeds and black peppercorns for 1-2 minutes. You will need to move the seeds around the skillet to ensure they are toasted evenly.
2. When the seeds are fragrant, remove the skillet from the heat.
3. Add the seeds to a grinder, and on a medium setting, pulverize. Transfer the seeds to a small bowl and add the remaining ingredients (dried chili flakes, salt, onion powder, and garlic powder). Set the mix aside.
4. Cut the lamb into 1.25-in (3.2-cm) cubes.
5. Add the lamb to a bowl and pour the spice mix over the meat, tossing to coat. Set the seasoned lamb aside for 15 minutes.
6. Before adding the meat to the preheated grill, oil the grill grates to ensure a nonstick surface.
7. Thread the cubes of lamb onto 6-8 metal skewers. You will need around 6-8 cubes per skewer.
8. Grill the kebabs for 10-12 minutes, flipping them over every 3 minutes.
9. Remove the lamb kebabs from the grill and enjoy.

CHAPTER-5 CHICKEN

· CUTS OF CHICKEN ·

BBQ CHICKEN WITH ASIAN DIPPING SAUCE

(TOTAL COOK TIME 2 HOURS 20 MINUTES)

INGREDIENTS FOR 3-4 SERVINGS

THE MEAT

- Olive oil or duck fat – 1 tablespoon
- 1 whole chicken, patted dry with kitchen paper
- BBQ rub, as needed

THE DIPPING SAUCE

- Mayonnaise - ⅓ cup
- Sweet chili sauce – 2 tablespoons
- Teriyaki sauce – 1 tablespoon
- Thai-style hot sauce – 1½ teaspoons
- Freshly ground black pepper – ¼ teaspoon
- Cilantro, chopped – 1 teaspoon

THE KAMADO GRILL

- Heat the Kamado grill for indirect heat and bring the temperature to 350°F (177°C)
- Use your favorite wood chunks for this recipe. Sassafras is a good choice

METHOD

1. Rub the olive oil or duck fat all over the chicken.
2. Scatter the BBQ rub all over the bird, and place on the grill.
3. While the chicken is cooking, in a bowl, combine the dipping sauce ingredients (mayonnaise, sweet chili sauce, teriyaki sauce, hot sauce, black pepper, and cilantro). Transfer the sauce to the fridge.
4. Cook the chicken until it registers an internal temperature of 160°F (70°C).
5. Remove the chicken from the grill and set aside to rest for 15 minutes until the temperature rises to 165°F (74°C).
6. Serve and enjoy.

CHICKEN SKEWERS

(TOTAL COOK TIME 1 HOUR 15 MINUTES)

INGREDIENTS FOR 2-4 SERVINGS

THE MEAT

- Boneless and skinless chicken breasts (1-lb, 0.45-kg)

THE MARINADE

- Peanut butter – 1 tablespoon
- Soy sauce – 2 tablespoons
- Freshly squeezed lemon juice – 2 tablespoons
- Sugar – ½ teaspoon
- 1 garlic clove, peeled and crushed
- Sweet BBQ sauce, store-bought – 1 tablespoon

THE KAMADO GRILL

- Heat the Kamado grill for direct cooking and place the grill rack in the upper position. The dome temperature needs to be around 450°F(250°C)
- Pre-soak bamboo skewers in water for 25-30 minutes before using

METHOD

1. Cut the chicken breast into bite-sized cubes.
2. Combine the peanut butter, soy sauce, fresh lemon juice, sugar, garlic, and sweet BBQ sauce in a bowl. Stir to combine, and add water if needed to achieve a smooth paste-like consistency.
3. Add the chicken to the bowl, and combine to coat evenly and well. Transfer the chicken to the refrigerator for a minimum of 30 minutes to marinate.
4. Remove the chicken from the fridge, shaking off any excess marinade.
5. Thread the chicken on the soaked skewers and cook on the cast iron plate, turning as needed until almost done. When around 99 percent cooked, remove the plate and complete the cooking process by placing directly on the grill. The process will take around 15-20 minutes. The chicken is ready when it registers an internal temperature of 165°F (74°C).
6. Remove from the grill, serve and enjoy.

GRILLED CHICKEN SALAD

(TOTAL COOK TIME 1 HOUR 40 MINUTES)

INGREDIENTS FOR 4 SERVINGS

THE MEAT

- 1 whole chicken, patted dry with kitchen paper
- Poultry rub, as needed

THE INGREDIENTS

- 4 celery stalks
- 4 green onions
- Green grapes, seedless – 1 cup
- Red grapes, seedless – 1 cup
- Fresh dill, chopped small, as needed

THE DRESSING

- Mayonnaise – ½ cup
- Sour cream – ½ cup
- 1 lemon, for juicing
- Brown sugar – 1-2 tablespoons
- Salt and freshly ground black pepper, to season
- Cumin, as needed

THE KAMADO GRILL

- Heat the Kamado grill for indirect heat and bring the temperature to 275-300°F (135-149°C)

METHOD

1. First, break the whole chicken down into breasts, wings, legs, and thighs.
2. Season the chicken pieces lightly with poultry rub.
3. Place the chicken on the grill and cook until the meat registers an internal temperature of 165°F (74°C). Remove the chicken from the grill and put to one side to cool.
4. Remove the bones from the chicken, discard along with the skin. Then, using two forks, shred the meat and set aside.
5. Next, chop the celery stalks into bite-size pieces.
6. Slice the tops off the onions, and chop.
7. Halve the green and red grapes.
8. Combine the celery, onions, and grapes in a bowl, and add the chopped fresh dill.
9. For the dressing, in a bowl, combine the mayonnaise and sour cream.
10. Squeeze the juice of 1 lemon into the mayo mixture and add 1-2 tablespoons of brown sugar to taste. Season the dressing with salt and black pepper.
11. Add the dressing to the veggies and grapes, gently stir to combine, and fold in the cumin.
12. Add the shredded chicken to the salad, and combine.

PISTACHIO CHICKEN

(TOTAL COOK TIME 1 HOUR 20 MINUTES)

INGREDIENTS FOR 2-3 SERVINGS

THE MEAT

- 2-3 large, skinless and boneless chicken breasts

THE INGREDIENTS

- Salted pistachios, coarsely chopped – ¾ cup
- Panko breadcrumbs – ¼ cup
- 1 egg
- Hot sauce – 3 tablespoons
- Onion powder – ¼ teaspoon
- Garlic powder – ¼ teaspoon
- Freshly ground black pepper – ¼ teaspoon
- Salt – ¼ teaspoon

THE KAMADO GRILL

- Heat the Kamado grill for indirect using the plate setter. It should be legs up with the grill grate on top of the legs. Preheat for 375°F (190°C)

METHOD

1. Rinse the chicken under cold running water, and then pat dry with kitchen paper towels.
2. Add the pistachios to a food processor, and on the pulse setting, process until coarsely chopped.
3. Transfer the nuts to a bowl, and stir in the breadcrumbs. Pour the mixture onto a plate.
4. In a second bowl, beat the egg and stir in the hot sauce. Add all of the dry ingredients (onion powder, garlic powder, pepper, and salt).
5. Dip the chicken breasts in the egg wash to cover completely. Next, dip in the nut and breadcrumb mixture, coating well.
6. Place the coated chicken breasts in the refrigerator for around 15 minutes to firm up the coating.
7. Remove the chicken breasts from the fridge, and slide them onto the grill grate. Cook the chicken for around 45 minutes until the meat registers an internal temperature of 165°F (74°C).
8. Serve and enjoy.

CHAPTER-6 TURKEY

· CUTS OF TURKEY ·

SMOKED TURKEY

(TOTAL COOK TIME 18 MINUTES)

INGREDIENTS FOR 6-8 SERVINGS

THE MEAT

- Pulled turkey, divided – 4 cups

THE INGREDIENTS

- Whole milk, divided – 3 cups
- All-purpose flour – 3 tablespoons
- Gouda cheese, shredded – 1 cup
- Smoked Cheddar cheese, shredded and divided – 2 cups
- Dry mustard – 1½ teaspoons
- Paprika – ½ tablespoons
- Kosher salt and ground pepper – ½ teaspoon each
- 1 package elbow macaroni, cooked al dente (1-lb, 0.45-kg)
- Green onion, chopped – 2 tablespoons

THE KAMADO GRILL

- Heat the Kamado grill for indirect grilling to 500°F (260°C)

METHOD

1. In a large pot, bring 2¾ cups milk to a low boil. Turn the heat down to moderately low.
2. Whisk the flour with the remaining milk in a small bowl until silky smooth. With a whisk, a little at a time, add the flour mixture to the hot milk for approximately 2 minutes until thickened. Gradually add the Gouda cheese, 1½ cups shredded Cheddar cheese, mustard, paprika, salt, and ground pepper. Stir until the cheeses are entirely melted, and remove the pan from the heat.
3. Add the cooked pasta along with 3 cups of pulled turkey to a Dutch oven.
4. Pour the cheese sauce over the top, followed by the remaining pulled turkey and Cheddar cheese. Bake until the cheese is melted, and the pasta mixture is browned lightly for around 5 minutes.
5. Garnish with green onions and enjoy.

SOUTHWEST-STYLE TURKEY BURGERS

(TOTAL COOK TIME 18 MINUTES)

INGREDIENTS FOR 4 SERVINGS

THE MEAT

- Ground turkey breast (1-lb, 0.45-kg)

THE INGREDIENTS

- Salsa - ⅓ cup
- Green onions, chopped – ¼ cup
- Dried oregano leaves – 1 teaspoon
- Ground cumin – ½ teaspoon
- Salt, as needed
- 1 small ripe avocado, peeled, pitted, and mashed
- Low-fat sour cream – 1 tablespoon
- Fresh cilantro, chopped – 1 tablespoon
- Freshly squeezed lime juice – 1 tablespoon
- 4 whole-wheat sandwich rolls, split
- 4 lettuce leaves
- 4 slices tomato

THE KAMADO GRILL

- Heat the Kamado grill for direct grilling to 450°F (232°C)

METHOD

1. In a bowl, combine the ground turkey, salsa, green onions, dried oregano leaves, ground cumin, and ¼ teaspoon of salt. Using clean hands, shape the mixture into 4 even-size patties.
2. Lay the patties on the grid and grill until cooked through, for around 4-5 minutes on each side.
3. In the meantime, in a bowl, combine avocado, sour cream, cilantro, and freshly squeezed lime juice. Season with salt and put to one side.
4. To each bottom half of roll, place a lettuce leaf followed by a turkey burger, tomatoes slices, and finally the avocado mixture.

TURKEY BACON DOGS

(TOTAL COOK TIME 15 MINUTES)

INGREDIENTS FOR 8 SERVINGS

THE MEAT

- 1 package turkey franks (1-lb, 0.45-kg)
- 8 rashers turkey bacon
- Nonstick cooking spray

THE INGREDIENTS

- 8 whole-wheat hot dog rolls, split
- Cheddar cheese, shredded ½-¾ cup
- Medium or hot salsa, store-bought
- Pickled jalapeno slices to serve
- Sour cream, to serve

THE KAMADO GRILL

- Spray the cold grill grate with nonstick cooking spray
- Heat the Kamado grill for direct grilling to 500°F (260°C)

METHOD

1. Wrap each frank with 1 turkey bacon slice.
2. Grill the franks while frequently turning until the turkey bacon is crispy.
3. Lay the franks in the hot dog rolls and scatter over the cheese.
4. Serve the franks with salsa, jalapeno pepper slices, and a dollop of sour cream.
5. Enjoy.

TURKEY POTATO SKINS

(TOTAL COOK TIME 1 HOUR 40 MINUTES)

INGREDIENTS FOR 6 SERVINGS

THE MEAT

- Turkey, cooked and chopped – 1 cup

THE INGREDIENTS

- 4 large russet potatoes, scrubbed
- Extra virgin olive oil, as needed
- Kosher salt, to season
- Cheddar cheese, grated (4-oz, 113-gm)
- 6 rashers bacon, cooked and crumbled
- Freshly ground black pepper, to season
- BBQ sauce, store-bought, as needed
- Sour cream – ½ cup
- 2 green onions, white and green parts, thinly sliced

THE KAMADO GRILL

- Heat the Kamado grill for direct grilling to 400°F (204°C)

METHOD

1. With a sharp-tipped knife, pierce the potatoes a few times and bake for 60 minutes, until fork-tender.
2. Remove the potatoes from the grill and set aside until cool enough to handle. Cut the potatoes horizontally in half, and with a spoon, scoop out the insides leaving around 0.25-in (0.64-cm) of potato flesh still on the skin.
3. Brush the potato skins with oil, both inside and out, and season with salt.
4. Cook the potatoes for 10 minutes on each side. Remove from the grill and set aside to cool.
5. In a bowl, combine the turkey, Cheddar cheese, and crumbled cooked bacon. Season with salt and black pepper to taste.
6. Stuff the turkey mixture into the skins, return them to the cooking grid, and bake for another 3-4 minutes until the cheese is bubbling. Remove the skins from the grill.
7. Drizzle BBQ sauce over the skins, and serve topped with sour cream and green onions.
8. Enjoy.

CHAPTER-7 FISH

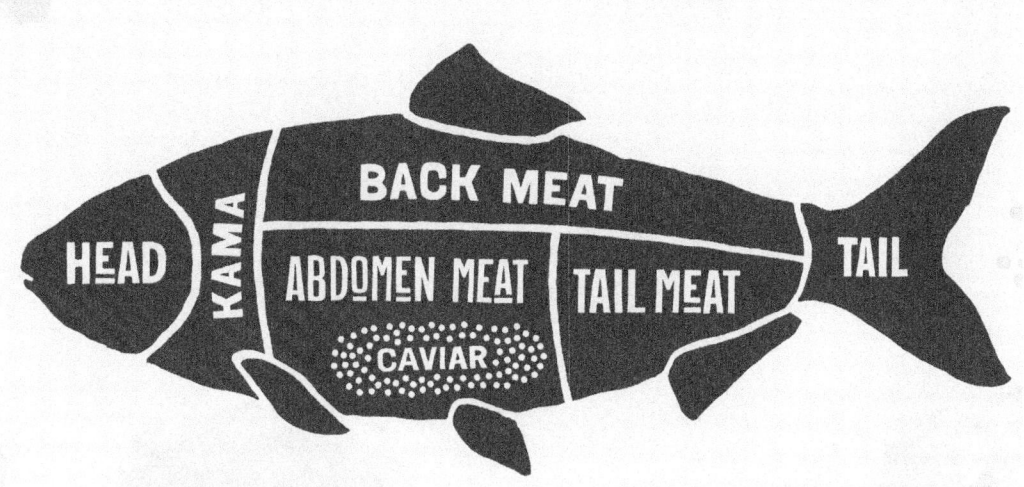

BLACKENED CAJUN CATFISH

(TOTAL COOK TIME 15 MINUTES)

INGREDIENTS FOR 4-6 SERVINGS

THE FISH

- 4-6 catfish fillets
- Avocado oil – 2 tablespoons
- Blackened Cajun seasoning, any brand, as needed – 3-4 tablespoons

THE KAMADO GRILL

- Heat the Kamado grill to 450°F (232°C)

METHOD

1. Coat the fish on both sides with avocado oil and season with blackened Cajun seasoning.
2. Lay the fish on the grill mat, and cook for around 6-8 minutes until pleasantly blackened. Then, flip the catfish over and cook for an additional 3-4 minutes.
3. Remove the fish from the grill and serve.

GRILLED ASIAN SALMON

(TOTAL COOK TIME 40 MINUTES)

INGREDIENTS FOR 2-4 SERVINGS

THE FISH

- 1 side of salmon, boneless, skin on (3-lb, 1.36-kg)

THE MARINADE

- Dijon mustard – 2 tablespoons
- Soy sauce – 3 tablespoons
- Olive oil, good quality – 6 tablespoons
- Garlic, peeled and minced – ½ teaspoon

THE KAMADO GRILL

- Heat the Kamado grill to high heat

METHOD

1. Place the fish, skin side facing down on a chopping board. Cut the fish crosswise into 4 even-sized portions.
2. In a bowl, whisk the mustard with soy sauce, olive oil, and garlic. Drizzle half of the marinade over the surface and set aside to rest for 10 minutes.
3. Remove the salmon from the marinade shaking off any excess. Set the remaining marinade to one side.
4. Lay the salmon skin side facing downwards on the preheated Kamado grill. Grill the salmon for 4-5 minutes, depending on its thickness. Then, flip over carefully and grill for an additional 4-5 minutes. At this stage, the fish will be slightly raw in the middle.
5. Transfer the salmon, skin side facing down, to a platter. Spoon the marinade over the top of the fish. Allow the salmon to rest for 10 minutes. Then, remove the skin and enjoy.

GRILLED RED SNAPPER IN BANANA LEAVES

(TOTAL COOK TIME 1 HOUR 30 MINUTES)

INGREDIENTS FOR 6 SERVINGS

THE FISH

- 6 boneless red snapper fillets (6-oz, 170-gm) each
- Salt and freshly ground black pepper to season
- Vegetable oil – 1 tablespoon
- Coarse sea salt – 1 teaspoon
- Freshly ground black pepper – ¼ teaspoon
- 2 large banana leaves, thawed
- Corn tortillas, as needed, to serve

THE MARINADE

- 2 guajillo chilies, seeded and stemmed
- Fresh orange juice – ½ cup
- Fresh lime juice – ½ cup
- White vinegar – 2 tablespoons
- Achiote paste (5-oz, 142-gm)
- 6 garlic cloves, peeled
- White onion, peeled and coarsely chopped - ¼ cup
- Sea salt and black pepper
- Ground allspice – ¼ teaspoon

THE KAMADO GRILL

- Heat the Kamado grill to moderate heat using the two-zone method. Alternatively, if the grill is gas, one side of the burners should be OFF, and the other should be ON

METHOD

1. Lay the fish fillets in a glass dish and season with salt and pepper.
2. For the marinade. In a frying pan, toast the chilies on both sides to release their oils without burning. Pour in sufficient water to cover and over moderate heat, simmer for around 15 minutes, to rehydrate, and soften. Set aside 2 tablespoons of rehydrated chili liquid.
3. In a food blender, add the now rehydrated chilies along with the chili water, fresh orange juice, lime juice, white vinegar, achiote paste, garlic, onion, sea salt, black pepper, and ground allspice. Process the ingredient until smooth.
4. Cover the red snapper fillets with the marinade to coat on both sides. Cover with kitchen wrap and transfer to the fridge to marinate for 1-12 hours.
5. Slice the banana leaves into 12-in (30.5-cm) squares.
6. Score the fish on both sides, rub with vegetable oil, and season with salt and pepper.
7. Lay the fillet on the center of the dull surface of the banana leaf. Fold up the bottom of the banana leaf to cover the fish. Next, fold in each side. Make one additional fold to create a package. Secure with butcher's twine.
8. Cook the fish parcels directly over the heat until charred on both sides. This will take around 3-4 minutes on each side.
9. Transfer the fish fillet to the indirect side of the grill and continue to cook until the fish registers an internal temperature of 140°F (60°C).
10. Serve the fish parcels with a stack of corn tortillas.
11. Enjoy.

MAHI MAHI

(TOTAL COOK TIME 1 HOUR 10 MINUTES)

INGREDIENTS FOR 2 SERVINGS

THE FISH

- Fresh mahi-mahi fillets (1-lb, 0.45-kg)
- Italian seasoning – ½ cup

THE KAMADO GRILL

- Heat the Kamado grill for direct cooking, with no heat deflector plates to 350°F (177°C)

METHOD

1. Add the fish to a plastic container with a lid.
2. Pour the Italian seasoning over the fish, and transfer it to the fridge for 60 minutes. Shake the container a couple of times during this time.
3. Grill the fish over the heat for 5 minutes on each side. The fish is ready when it flakes easily when using a fork.
4. Enjoy.

CHAPTER-8 SEAFOOD

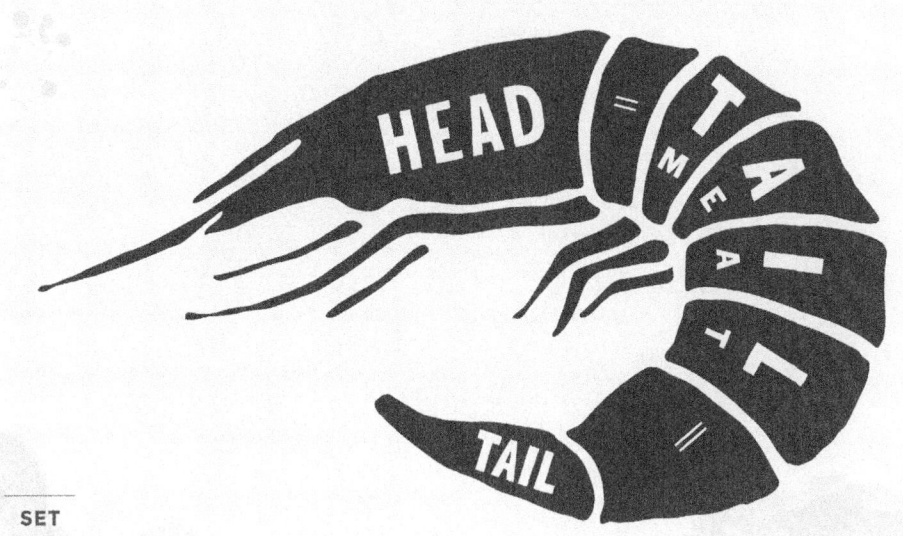

BBQ SHRIMP SALAD

(TOTAL COOK TIME 25 MINUTES)

INGREDIENTS FOR 4-5 SERVINGS

THE SEAFOOD

- Shrimp, peeled and deveined (1-lb, 0.45-kg)

THE INGREDIENTS

- 4 corn cobs, peeled
- Extra-virgin olive oil, as needed
- Honey chipotle rub, store-bought, as needed
- Ranch dressing - ⅔ cup
- BBQ sauce, of choice - ⅓ cup
- Freshly cracked black pepper, to taste
- Chives, chopped, to taste
- A head of iceberg lettuce, thinly sliced
- Grape tomatoes, halved – ½ cup
- 1 red onion, peeled and diced
- 2 avocadoes, peeled, pitted, and diced
- A small bunch of basil, chiffonade
- 4-6 radishes, thinly sliced
- 1 fresh lime, cut into quarters

THE KAMADO GRILL

- Heat the Kamado grill for direct grilling to high heat
- You will need double-pronged metal skewers for this recipe

METHOD

1. Skewer the shrimp onto double-pronged metal skewers
2. Brush the surface of the corn cobs with olive oil.
3. Season the corn cobs and shrimp with honey chipotle rub, and set aside for 10-15 minutes before grilling over direct and high heat.
4. Grill the corn cobs until heated through and char marks appear. Grill the shrimp for 2-3 minutes until opaque and cooked through.
5. Meanwhile, in a bowl, whisk the ranch dressing with the BBQ sauce. Taste the mixture and adjust the ratio of dressing and sauce as needed. Season with black pepper and chopped chives.
6. Remove the kernels from the grilled corn.
7. In a bowl, combine the lettuce, tomatoes, red onion, avocado, basil, radishes, and lime wedges. Fold in any remaining dressing and top with juicy grilled shrimp.
8. Enjoy.

LOBSTER ROLLS

(TOTAL COOK TIME 35 MINUTES)

INGREDIENTS FOR 6 SERVINGS

THE SEAFOOD

- 3 lobster tails approx. (8-oz, 226-gm) each

THE INGREDIENTS

- Salt and black pepper, to season
- Butter, divided – 4 tablespoons
- Garlic powder, as needed
- 6 buns, split, to serve
- Spinach leaves, as needed, to serve
- Avocado, peeled, pitted, and sliced, to serve

THE KAMADO GRILL

- Heat the Kamado grill for indirect grilling to 350°F (177°C)

METHOD

1. Split the top of the lobster shells and pull the meat out to rest on the top.
2. Make 2-3 slits in the lobster meat to ensure an even cook and place on a perforated cooking grid. Season the lobster meat with salt and black pepper.
3. In a small bowl, combine 2 tablespoons of butter with a pinch of garlic powder.
4. Brush the garlic butter generously over the lobster tails.
5. Place the lobster tails in the Kamado grill and cook for around 25 minutes, or until the tails are firm to the touch. Remove from the grill and allow to cool.
6. Next, cook the lobster tails over direct heat.
7. Melt the remaining butter and a pinch of garlic powder in a small bowl, and brush over the sides of the rills. Grill the buns for 2-3 minutes on each side until golden.
8. Remove the meat from the lobster shells and cut into large dice. Add to the dressing and mix thoroughly to combine.
9. Place a few spinach leaves on each bun. Follow with 2-3 slices of avocado and top each serving with an even amount of the lobster mix.

NEW ENGLAND STYLE CLAM CHOWDER

(TOTAL COOK TIME 45 MINUTES)

INGREDIENTS FOR 8 SERVINGS

THE SEAFOOD

- 1 jar clam juice (8-oz, 227-gm)
- 2 cans chopped clams, drained (6.5-oz, 184-gm) each
- 1 can baby clams, drained (10-oz, 284-gm)

THE INGREDIENTS

- Baby yellow potatoes, halved (1-lb, 0.45-kg)
- 1 large onion (peeled, sliced thick)
- 1 large red bell pepper, halved and seeded
- Bacon, thick-cut, diced (8-oz, 227-gm)
- 2-3 celery stalks, trimmed and diced
- 3 garlic cloves, peeled and minced
- Tri-tip seasoning, as needed
- 1 bay leaf
- 3 thyme sprigs
- Chicken stock – 1 cup
- Pizza flour, "OO" – ¼ cup
- Heavy cream – 2 cups

THE KAMADO GRILL

- Build a large hot coal bed in your Kamado grill and set up for direct grilling. Positing the grates in the lowest position of the divide and conquer system, with the airflow wide open

METHOD

1. Add the potatoes, onion, and bell pepper to the grill. Grill, with the lid open, until the veggies are charred. Remove the veggies from the grill.
2. Close the airflow and stabilize the grill to a temperature of 450°F (232°C).
3. Place a Dutch oven of 20 cup capacity in the grill, and preheat.
4. Cook the bacon in the Dutch oven, and cook until beginning to brown and crisp. Put the bacon aside, and pour away all but 2 tablespoons of bacon drippings.
5. Meanwhile, dice the veggies.
6. Add the onion and celery to the Dutch oven and cook until the onions start to soften and become translucent. Next, add the potatoes, bell pepper, garlic, and tri-tip seasoning. Cook for approximately 60 seconds until the garlic is fragrant.
7. Using kitchen twine, tie the bay leaf, and thyme sprigs in a bundle. Add to the Dutch oven followed by the clam juice from both the bottle and canned clams.
8. Pour in the stock, flour, and cream, and bring to a simmer.
9. Cook until the potatoes are fork-tender, for around 10-15 minutes.
10. Add the clams to the chowder, and cook for an additional 5 minutes. Remove from the grill, stir in the bacon.
11. Serve and enjoy.

SMOKED CRAB DIP

(TOTAL COOK TIME 25 MINUTES)

INGREDIENTS FOR 6 SERVINGS

THE SEAFOOD

- Crabmeat (1-lb, 0.45-kg)

THE INGREDIENTS

- Cream cheese (3-lb, 1.36-kg)
- Seafood rub, store-bought, of choice – 1 tablespoon
- Garlic, peeled and minced – 1½ tablespoons
- Fresh parsley, chopped – 2 tablespoons
- Freshly squeezed juice of 2 lemons
- Sriracha – ½ teaspoon
- Parmesan cheese, finely grated – 1 cup
- 1 lemon, cut into wedges

THE KAMADO GRILL

- Heat the Kamado grill to 300°F (149°C)
- Place the soapstone on the highest heat setting with one grill grate

METHOD

1. Add the cream cheese to a bowl, and smooth out to create the maximum surface area. Place the bowl on the grill and close the lid. Smoke for 3-5 minutes, and bring to temperature.
2. Remove the cream cheese from the Kamado grill, and fold in the seafood rub, garlic, crab meat, parsley, freshly squeezed lemon juice, Sriracha, and ½ cup of Parmesan cheese.
3. Transfer the mixture to a cast-iron skillet and top with the remaining finely grated Parmesan cheese.
4. Set the grill grates on divide and conquer system the lowest setting. Put the soapstone on the highest setting.
5. Place the dip on the grill grate, under the soapstone. Close the lid and cook for 6-10 minutes. The dip is ready to enjoy when the cheese is browned slightly.
6. Garnish with the remaining parsley, and garnish with wedges of lemon.
7. Serve with toasted pita, and enjoy.

CHAPTER-9 GAME

BEAR BURGERS

(TOTAL COOK TIME 30 MINUTES)

INGREDIENTS FOR 8 SERVINGS

THE GAME

- Ground bear meat (2-lb, 0.9-kg)
- Hamburger seasoning, as needed
- Parmesan cheese, grated
- 8 hamburger buns, split

THE KAMADO GRILL

- Heat the Kamado grill to 375°F (190°C)

METHOD

1. Add the ground bear meat to a bowl. Season generously and scatter over enough grated cheese to cover completely. Knead to combine evenly.
2. Divide the meat mixture into 8 even-size portions.
3. Cook the burgers on the preheated grill until the meat registers an internal temperature of 170°F (77°C) for around 20-25 minutes.
4. Toast the buns.
5. Serve the burgers inside buns topped with your favorite fixings.
6. Enjoy.

GRILLED HONEY-GLAZE CORNISH HENS

(TOTAL COOK TIME 1 HOUR 35 MINUTES)

INGREDIENTS FOR 8 SERVINGS

THE GAME

- 2 Cornish hens, rinsed and patted dry
- Butter– 2 tablespoons
- Honey – 3 tablespoons
- Sea salt – ¼ teaspoon
- Cracked black pepper – ¼ teaspoon
- Paprika – ¼ teaspoon

THE KAMADO GRILL

- Heat the Kamado grill for indirect cooking to 375°F (190°C)

METHOD

1. First, spatchcock the hens. Then, using kitchen scissors, cut up each side of the bird's backbone from back to front to remove. Bend the hens in half and lay skin side facing upwards.
2. Melt the butter, and combine thoroughly with honey. Apply the mixture generously to the surface of the birds.
3. In a small bowl, combine the salt, pepper, and paprika and scatter the mixture over the skin side of the hens.
4. When the heat is at the desired temperature, lay the hens directly on the grill grate, skin side facing upwards. Cook the hens until the internal temperature registers an internal temperature of 165°F (74°C). This step will take around 1 hour 20 minutes. Set aside to rest for 5 minutes before serving.

HONEY-ORANGE MARINADED GATOR KEBABS

(TOTAL COOK TIME 24 HOURS 25 MINUTES)

INGREDIENTS FOR 4 SERVINGS

THE GAME

- Alligator meat, cut into 1-in (2.54-cm) cubes, total weight (1-lb, 0.45-kg)

THE KEBABS

- Cherry tomatoes, as needed
- Bell peppers, cut into chunks, as needed
- Sweet onions, as needed
- Creole seasoning, to taste

THE MARINADE

- Frozen orange juice concentrate – 5 tablespoons
- Orange juice, pulp-free - ⅔ cup
- Honey – 7 tablespoons
- Orange zest, grated – 1¼ teaspoons
- 1 large garlic clove, peeled and minced
- Salt - ⅔ teaspoon
- Crushed red pepper – 1½ teaspoons

THE KAMADO GRILL

- Heat the Kamado grill to moderate heat
- You will need 4 metal skewers for this recipe

METHOD

1. In a bowl, combine the marinade ingredients (orange juice concentrate, orange juice, honey, orange zest, garlic cloves, salt, and red pepper).
2. Add the cubes of meat to the marinade and transfer to the fridge for a minimum of 24 hours.
3. Thread the cubes of gator onto metal skewers alternating with cherry tomatoes, bell peppers, and sweet onion.
4. Baste the kebabs with any remaining marinade and season to taste with Creole seasoning.
5. Cook the kebabs until the peppers are cooked but not crunchy.

SMOKED GOOSE

(TOTAL COOK TIME 3 HOURS 30 MINUTES)

INGREDIENTS FOR 2-3 SERVINGS

THE GAME

- 1 small wild goose
- Salt, as needed
- Thick maple syrup – ¼ cup

THE RUB

- Sugar – 1 tablespoon
- Salt – 1 teaspoon
- Freshly ground black pepper – 1 teaspoon
- Chinese 5-spice powder – ½ teaspoon
- Ground coriander – ½ teaspoon
- Ground cinnamon – ¼ teaspoon
- Sesame oil – 1 tablespoon

THE SMOKING MIXTURE

- Cherry wood smoking chips – 2 cups
- White rice – ½ cup
- Black tea, brewed – ½ cup
- Brown sugar – ½ cup
- 3 cinnamon sticks
- 3 star anise
- 3 strips orange peel

THE KAMADO GRILL

- Heat the Kamado grill to 300°F (149°C)
- You will need to prepare your own smoking mixture for this recipe (see below)

METHOD

1. Rinse the bird inside and out and pat dry.
2. First, prepare the rub: In a bowl, combine the sugar, salt, black pepper, Chinese 5-spice, coriander, and cinnamon, and stir to incorporate.
3. Season the front and main cavity of the bird with half of the rub. Brush the surface of the bird with sesame oil.
4. Scatter the remaining rub over all the bird, rubbing it gently into the skin.
5. Prick the bird's skin all over to help the fat escape and give the skin a crispy texture.
6. Prepare the smoking mixture by combining the cherry wood chips, white rice, black tea, brown sugar, cinnamon stick, star anise, and orange peel. Stir to incorporate.
7. Place the bird on the rack and the drip pan on the deflector plate. Add around half of the smoking mixture to the smoking chamber and smoke for 2 hours until it registers an internal temperature of 145°F (63°C).
8. Increase the heat to 350°F (177°C).
9. Brush the fat from the drip pan all over the bird.
10. Add the remaining smoking mixture and continue to smoke until the skin is crisp and dark and the meat registers an internal temperature of 175-180°F (79-82°C) for an additional 60-90 minutes.

CHAPTER-10 VEGGIES

BACON-WRAPPED ONION RINGS

(TOTAL COOK TIME 35 MINUTES)

INGREDIENTS FOR 4-5 SERVINGS

THE VEGGIES

- 2 large yellow onions, sliced into 1-in (2.54-cm) rings

THE INGREDIENTS

- Regular-cut bacon slices (2-lb, 0.9-kg)
- BBQ sauce, store-bought, as needed
- Jalapeno honey mustard, store-bought, as needed, optional, to serve

THE KAMADO GRILL

- Build a coal bed and set the Kamado grill for indirect grilling with deflector plates. Stabilize the temperature to 325°F (163°C)

METHOD

1. Double up the onion ring slices to create a thick onion ring.
2. Wrap bacon around the 2 onion slices to cover completely.
3. Brush BBQ sauce over the rings and place in a single layer on the grill grates. Cook for approximately 30 minutes, until the bacon, is browned and cooked.
4. Brush the surface of the bacon once again, and remove from the Kamado grill.
5. Serve with jalapeno honey mustard and enjoy.

BRUSSELS SPROUTS AU GRATIN

(TOTAL COOK TIME 45 MINUTES)

INGREDIENTS FOR 10 SERVINGS

THE VEGGIES

- Brussels sprouts, trimmed and halved (2-lb, 0.9-kg)

THE INGREDIENTS

- Pancetta, diced (4-oz, 113-gm)
- 2 shallots, thinly sliced
- 4 garlic cloves, peeled and minced
- Thyme leaves – 1 tablespoon
- Extra-virgin olive oil – 3 tablespoons
- All-purpose seasoning – 2 tablespoons
- Heavy cream – 2 cups
- Dijon mustard – 2 tablespoons
- Gruyere cheese, finely grated (2-oz, 57-gm)
- Parmigiano Reggiano, finely grated (4-oz, 113-gm)
- Panko breadcrumbs – 1 cup

THE KAMADO GRILL

- Preheat your Kamado grill and a cast-iron 10-in (25.4-cm) skillet to 400°F (204°C)

METHOD

1. Once the skillet is hot, add the diced pancetta and cook until the meat is brown and the fat rendered.
2. Add the sprouts, shallots, garlic, thyme, olive oil, and all-purpose seasoning to the skillet, and toss to mix.
3. Close the grill and cook the Brussels sprouts for around 40-45 minutes, until brown and softened.
4. In a bowl, whisk together the cream and mustard. Pour the mixture over the sprouts. Scatter over the breadcrumbs and continue to cook until the gratin is bubbling and the topping is golden. This will take approximately half an hour.
5. Take off the grill and enjoy.

CREAMY CHEESE POTATO SALAD

(TOTAL COOK TIME 40 MINUTES)

INGREDIENTS FOR 4 SERVINGS

THE VEGGIES

- Fingerling potatoes (5-lb, 2.27-kg)

THE INGREDIENTS

- Nonstick vegetable oil spray
- Tri-tip seasoning, as needed
- Feta, crumbled – ½ cup
- Dill pickles from jar, diced – ½ cup
- Chives, minced – ¼ cup

THE DRESSING

- Mayonnaise – 1 cup
- Sour cream – 1 cup
- Boursin cheese – ¾ cup
- Parsley leaves – 1 cup
- Baby dill, minced – ½ cup
- Tarragon leaves – 2 tablespoons
- Dill pickle juice, from jar – 2 tablespoons
- Garlic, peeled and minced – 1 teaspoon
- Black pepper, to season
- Smoked salt, to season

THE KAMADO GRILL

- Preheat your Kamado grill for direct grilling to 500°F (260°C)

METHOD

1. Place the potatoes on the grill and cook for 10 minutes, or until charred on both sides.
2. Remove the potatoes from the Kamado grill and place in a Dutch oven.
3. Close the airflow and stabilize the grill temperature to 400°F (204°C).
4. Spritz the potatoes with nonstick vegetable oil, season with tri-tip seasoning, and toss to evenly and well coat. Cover the grill with its lid and place the Dutch oven on the grill.
5. Cook the potatoes until tender, for around 20-30 minutes. Remove from the grill and transfer to a shallow pan to cool in the fridge. Dice the potatoes into bite-size pieces.
6. For the dressing, in a food blender or processor, combine the mayonnaise, sour cream, Boursin cheese, parsley leaves, baby dill, tarragon leaves, pickle juice, garlic, and black pepper. Season to taste with smoked salt.
7. Toss the potatoes with the homemade dressing and serve cold, topped with feta cheese, dill pickles, and minced chives.

GRILLED ARTICHOKES WITH LEMON DILL YOGURT SAUCE

(TOTAL COOK TIME 35 MINUTES)

INGREDIENTS FOR 4-6 SERVINGS

THE VEGGIES

- 4-6 artichokes

THE INGREDIENTS

- 1 lemon, halved
- Extra-virgin olive oil - ⅔ cup
- Fresh lemon juice - ⅓ cup
- Citrus and herb seasoning, any brand, to season
- Salt and freshly ground black pepper, to season, optional

THE SAUCE

- Plain, low-fat Greek yogurt – 1 cup
- Fresh dill, chopped – 2 tablespoons
- Lemon zest – 2 teaspoons
- Freshly squeezed lemon juice – 1 tablespoon
- Extra-virgin olive oil – 1 tablespoon

THE KAMADO GRILL

- Heat the Kamado grill for indirect grilling to 450°F (232°C)

METHOD

1. Fill a large bowl with cold water, squeeze in the fresh juice of ½ lemon, and add the other ½ lemon to the bowl.
2. Snip the tips off the artichoke leaves, and then cut each artichoke in half through the stem, lengthwise. Scoop out the choke and add the artichoke to the water-filled bowl while you prepare the remaining artichokes.
3. Bring a large pot of salted water to a boil.
4. Drain the artichokes, add them to the pot and boil for 20-25 minutes, until just tender. Drain well and allow to cool.
5. In a small bowl, whisk the oil with ⅓ cup fresh lemon juice and add citrus herb seasoning to taste. Season with salt and black pepper, if necessary.
6. Brush the artichokes with the dressing and lay them face downwards on the grill grid. Grill the veggies until charred lightly in spots while occasionally turning for around 7-8 minutes. Transfer the artichokes to a serving platter.
7. In the meantime, prepare the yogurt sauce. In a bowl, combine the sauce ingredients (yogurt, fresh dill, lemon zest, lemon juice, and olive oil).
8. Remove the artichokes from the Kamado grill and serve with the lemon-dill yogurt sauce.
9. Enjoy.

MEXICAN STREET CORN

(TOTAL COOK TIME 30 MINUTES)

INGREDIENTS FOR 4 SERVINGS

THE VEGGIES

- 4 corn ears

THE INGREDIENTS

- Mayonnaise – 1½ cups
- Sour cream – 1½ cups
- Cilantro, freshly chopped – ¼ cup
- Freshly squeezed juice of 1 lime
- Freshly squeezed juice of 1 lemon
- Cilantro paste – 3 tablespoons
- Smoked paprika – 2 teaspoons
- Sriracha hot sauce – ¼ cup
- Mexican seasoning – ¼ cup
- Mexican blend cheese, freshly grated – 1 cup

THE KAMADO GRILL

- Preheat your Kamado grill to 350°F (177°C)

METHOD

1. Combine the mayonnaise, sour cream, cilantro, lime juice, lemon juice, cilantro paste, paprika, hot sauce, and Mexican seasoning in a bowl.
2. Cook the corn ears on the grill for 25 minutes, flipping them over every 5-7 minutes.
3. Remove the corn ears from the Kamado grill.
4. Slather the mayonnaise mixture over each corn ear to coat.
5. Scatter the Mexican cheese over the corn ears, and enjoy.

CHAPTER-11 CERAMIC GILL

DIFFERENT SIZES OF KAMADO GRILLS

You should be aware that there are a number of different sizes that are available for you to purchase. The following section should give you a small breakdown of the different sizes that are available to you.

1) **Mini:** This model is the absolutely perfect for those individuals who want to carry it to a picnic or have a small home. This unit weighs about 36 pounds and has a grid diameter of 10 inches. It has the capacity to hold about 2 chicken breasts in one go.

2) **MiniMax:** This particular model is also awesome for camping and small parties. It is easy to carry and comes with a nifty and sturdy grip. It weighs 90 pounds and has a diameter of 13 inches. It can hold a 12 pounds turkey in one go.

3) **Small:** This is perfect for individuals who have a small sized balcony or as an additional kamado to another large kamado. It weighs about 80 pounds and has a diameter of 13 inches. It can cook a turkey of about 12 pounds. It is pretty portable and compatible with half moon raised grid, round grill work and jalapeno grill rack.

4) **Medium:** This model is ideal for couples and new small families. Most accessories are supported by this model and it weighs about 113 pounds. It sports a diameter of 15 inches and can accommodate a turkey of 18 pounds. Best accessories for this model would be cast iron cooking grid, grid cleaner, vertical chicken roaster etc.

5) **Large:** This one the most optimal size for moderately large sized families and most gatherings. It supports most accessories as well and has a diameter of 18.25 inches with 162 pounds weight. It can hold a 20 pounds turkey and supports most accessories such as the deep dish aking stone, v rack and so on.

6) **X-Large:** This particular model is best suited for large families and large friend gatherins. It allows for many meals to be cooked at same time, in fact twelve racks of ribs and 24 burgers can be made in a single session. It weights about 219 pounds and has a grid diameter of 24 inches. It has the capacity to hold 20 pound turkeys and can be used with, pizza peel and baking stone.

7) **XX-Large:** This is the largest one of the bunch! It is not only suitable for large family, but perfect for large parties and commercial usage, and therefore should be considered for catering groups or restaurants.

Ceramic Grill Tips

There are certain things that you should know about as they will help you to enjoy the early days of your kamado even more.

1) When using a kamado, always make sure to keep it on flat, leveled surface
2) The kamado's are designed to be used with a metal nest, ensuring a gap between the kamado and the bottom to allow air flow. Even if you are not using a nest, make sure to set it up in such a way that the air flow does not get obstructed.
3) Make sure to never keep yourkamado on flammable surface
4) Never leave the dome opened
5) It case there are high-winds, it is highly advised that you keep a close look at your kamado while during the cooking session in order to prevent any mishaps
6) When firing up your kamado for the first time, try to prevent the kamado from reaching temperatures higher than 350 degrees F, as it will help the gasket adhesive to cure
7) Make sure to never use fluid lighter to light up your kamado. These chemicals will greatly alter the flavor of your food. Instead, try opting for BGE electric charcoal starter to light up your charcoals
8) When you are moving your kamado, first make sure that your kamado is complete cool. Never try to move a warm/hot kamado as it might cause harm to you.
9) When cooking at temperatures above 400 degrees F, try to ensure that you lift the lid about 1-2 inches prior to opening it up completely. This allows a little amount of heat to escape and prevent any self injury, this process is also known as "Burping"

Cooking Types

Direct Grilling

When talking about direct grilling, we are basically placing the directly over fire and cooking it by exposing it to heat and flame. It's pretty much the perfect way to cook chops, steaks, chicken breast, burgers, fillets, veggies and other simple and quick to cook foods. Basically, foods that are just tender and have a thickness of less than 2 inch are perfect for grilling directly. When you are grilling directly, you should know that it slowly sears the outer surface of your meat and forms a fine yet satisfying crust, keeping all the juices perfectly locked inside giving an amazing flavor. In fact, the meticulously designed kamado ensures that you don't get any hot spots or flare ups too! Keep in mind though, that for some food, you might need to start direct grilling at a high temperature and then lower down the heat as you go by.

Indirect Grilling

When you are considering Indirect Grilling, you are essentially cooking the food using a drip pan, ensuring that the ingredient is not directly exposed to flame, but is rather cooked by heat produced at the bottom of the pan. To be more scientific, the food is cooked via convection that allows heat to radiate from the coal and dome of the kamado. This allows you to prepare rotisserie as well, as it allows the appliance rotisserie cooking as well.

SMOKING

Following the tradition, it is actually possible to Smoke meals using your kamado grill. Smoking using your kamado allows you to cook your meals slowly and infuse them with the smoky flavors of the wood that you are using. It allows you to slowly break down the tissues and make the meat very tender. Smoking requires a long time, for some foods smoking is done in a matter of mere minutes while for others it might take hours upon hours. The result however, would always be extremely satisfying, literally fall-off-the bone type meat with a combination of complex flavors generated by the smoke and spices that you use. Aside from the usual meat though, using the kamado you can also smoke various other types of food such as nuts, veggies, cheese and even nuts. The recommended temperature for smoking using the kamado falls somewhere around 225 degrees F to about 275 degrees F. The perfectly designed dome of the kamado makes it easier for pit masters to adjust the openings that allows for Smoke cooking.

BAKING

This is something that most people don't know about, but kamado actually allows you to use the kamado as a classical brick oven that allows you to use the kamado to make pies, biscuits, bread, pizza as so on. With absolutely precise temperature controls and heat holding capacities, it is possible to turn the kamado into the perfect baking stone! The DOME shape further helps to create a fine environment for baking while the material helps to draw the moisture and create extra-ordinary dishes!

CHAPTER-12 SMOKING TIPS AND TRICKS

SELECTING A SMOKER

You need to invest in a good smoker if you are going to smoke meat on a regular basis. Consider these options when buying a smoker. Here are two natural fire option for you:

- Charcoal smokers are fueled by a combination of charcoal and wood. Charcoal burns easily and the temperature remains steady, so you won't have any problem with a charcoal smoker. The wood gives a great flavor to the meat and you will enjoy smoking meats.
- Wood smoker: The wood smoker will give your brisket and ribs the best smoky flavor and taste, but it is a bit harder to cook with wood. Both hardwood blocks and chips are used as fuel.

CHOOSE YOUR WOOD

You need to choose your wood carefully because the type of wood you will use affect greatly to the flavor and taste of the meat. Here are a few options for you:

- Maple: Maple has a smoky and sweet taste and goes well with pork or poultry
- Alder: Alder is sweet and light. Perfect for poultry and fish.
- Apple: Apple has a mild and sweet flavor. Goes well with pork, fish, and poultry.
- Oak: Oak is great for slow cooking. Ideal for game, pork, beef, and lamb.
- Mesquite: Mesquite has a smoky flavor and extremely strong. Goes well with pork or beef.
- Hickory: Has a smoky and strong flavor. Goes well with beef and lamb.
- Cherry: Has a mild and sweet flavor. Great for pork, beef, and turkey

Wood Type	Fish	Chicken	Beef	Pork
Apple	Yes	Yes	No	No
Alder	Yes	Yes	No	Yes
Cherry	Yes	Yes	Yes	Yes
Hickory	No	No	Yes	Yes
Maple	No	Yes	No	No
Mulberry	Yes	Yes	No	Yes
Mesquite	No	No	Yes	Yes
Oak	Yes	Yes	Yes	Yes
Pecan	No	Yes	Yes	Yes
Pear	No	Yes	No	Yes
Peach	No	Yes	No	Yes
Walnut	No	No	Yes	Yes

Find the right temperature

- Start at 250F (120C): Start your smoker a bit hot. This extra heat gets the smoking process going.

- Temperature drop: Once you add the meat to the smoker, the temperature will drop, which is fine.

- Maintain the temperature. Monitor and maintain the temperature. Keep the temperature steady during the smoking process.

Avoid peeking every now and then. Smoke and heat two most important element make your meat taste great. If you open the cover every now and then you lose both of them and your meat loses flavor. Only the lid only when you truly need it.

The core difference between cold and hot smoking

Depending on the type of grill that you are using, you might be able to get the option to go for a Hot Smoking Method or a Cold Smoking One. The primary fact about these three different cooking techniques which you should keep in mind are as follows:

- **Hot Smoking:** In this technique, the food will use both the heat on your grill and the smoke to prepare your food. This method is most suitable for items such as chicken, lamb, brisket etc.
- **Cold Smoking:** In this method, you are going to smoke your meat at a very low temperature such as 30 degree Celsius, making sure that it doesn't come into the direct contact with the heat. This is mostly used as a means to preserve meat and extend their life on the shelf.
- **Roasting Smoke:** This is also known as Smoke Baking. This process is essentially a combined form of both roasting and baking and can be performed in any type of smoker with a capacity of reaching temperatures above 82 degree Celsius.

THE BASIC PREPARATIONS

- Always be prepared to spend the whole day and take as much time as possible to smoke your meat for maximum effect.
- Make sure to obtain the perfect Ribs/Meat for the meal which you are trying to smoke. Do a little bit of research if you need.
- I have already added a list of woods in this book, consult to that list and choose the perfect wood for your meal.
- Make sure to prepare the marinade for each of the meals properly. A great deal of the flavor comes from the rubbing.
- Keep a meat thermometer handy to get the internal temperature when needed.
- Use mittens or tongs to keep yourself safe
- Refrain yourself from using charcoal infused alongside starter fluid as it might bring a very unpleasant odor to your food
- Always make sure to start off with a small amount of wood and keep adding them as you cook.
- Don't be afraid to experiment with different types of wood for newer flavor and experiences.
- Always keep a notebook near you and note jot down whatever you are doing or learning and use them during the future session. This will help you to evolve and move forward.

THE CORE ELEMENTS OF SMOKING!

Smoking is a very indirect method of cooking that relies on a number of different factors to give you the most perfectly cooked meal that you are looking for. Each of these components is very important to the whole process as they all work together to create the meal of your dreams.

- **Time**: Unlike grilling or even Barbequing, smoking takes a really long time and requires a whole lot of patience. It takes time for the smoky flavor to slowly get infused into the meats. Jus to bring things into comparison, it takes an about 8 minutes to fully cook a steak through direct heating, while smoking (indirect heating) will take around 35-40 minutes.
- **Temperature:** When it comes to smoking, the temperature is affected by a lot of different factors that are not only limited to the wind, cold air temperatures but also the cooking wood's dryness. Some smokers work best with large fires that are controlled by the draw of a chimney and restricted airflow through the various vents of the cooking chamber and firebox. While other smokers tend to require smaller fire with fewer coals as well as a completely different combination of the vent and draw controls. However, most smokers are designed to work at temperatures as low as 180 degrees Fahrenheit to as high as 300 degrees Fahrenheit. But the recommend temperature usually falls between 250 degrees Fahrenheit and 275 degrees Fahrenheit.
- **Airflow:** The level of air to which the fire is exposed to greatly determines how your fire will burn and how quickly it will burn the fuel. For instance, if you restrict air flow into the firebox by closing up the available vents, then the fire will burn at a low temperature and vice versa. Typically in smokers, after lighting up the fire, the vents are opened to allow for maximum airflow and is then adjusted throughout the cooking process to make sure that optimum flame is achieved.
- **Insulation:** Insulation is also very important when it comes to smokers as it helps to easily manage the cooking process throughout the whole cooking session. A good insulation allows smokers to efficiently reach the desired temperature instead of waiting for hours upon hours!

CONCLUSION

The book includes smoked meat recipes comprising beef, fish, seafood, pork, ham, lamb, poultry, vegetables, and game. If you want to just treat yourself to mouthwatering, perfectly cooked smoked meat or entertain family or friends, this book will provide everything you need.

MY BOOKS

https://www.amazon.com/dp/B08PJK7CKX

https://www.amazon.com/dp/B08P6DTTNB

https://www.amazon.com/dp/B08NVCQHM8

https://www.amazon.com/dp/B08M8DBJSF

https://www.amazon.com/dp/1797805525

https://www.amazon.com/dp/B08FSKQCY9

Copyright 2021©   Roger Murphy

All rights reserved. No part of this guide may be reproduced in any form without permission in writing from the publisher except in the case of brief quotations embodied in critical articles or reviews.

Legal & Disclaimer*: The information contained in this book and its contents is not designed to replace or take the place of any form of medical or professional advice; and is not meant to replace the need for independent medical, financial, legal or other professional advice or services, as may be required. The content and information in this book have been provided for educational and entertainment purposes only.*

The content and information contained in this book have been compiled from sources deemed reliable, and it is accurate to the best of the Author's knowledge, information, and belief. However, the Author cannot guarantee its accuracy and validity and cannot be held liable for any errors and/or omissions. Further, changes are periodically made to this book as and when needed. Where appropriate and/or necessary, you must consult a professional (including but not limited to your doctor, attorney, financial advisor or such other professional advisor) before using any of the suggested remedies, techniques, or information in this book.

Upon using the contents and information contained in this book, you agree to hold harmless the Author from and against any damages, costs, and expenses, including any legal fees potentially resulting from the application of any of the information provided by this book. This disclaimer applies to any loss, damages or injury caused by the use and application, whether directly or indirectly, of any advice or information presented, whether for breach of contract, tort, negligence, personal injury, criminal intent, or under any other cause of action.

P.S. Thank you for reading this book. If you've enjoyed this book, please don't shy, drop me a line, leave a feedback or both on Amazon. I love reading feedbacks and your opinion is extremely important for me.

GET YOUR FREE GIFT

Subscribe to our Mail List and get your FREE copy of the book

'Smoking Meat: The Best 20 Recipes of Smoked Meat, Unique Recipes for Unique BBQ'

https://tiny.cc/smoke20

Printed in Great Britain
by Amazon